DISCARD

D1710780

12 IMMIGRANTS WHO MADE
AMERICAN
SPORTS GREAT

by Janet Slingerland

12 STORY LIBRARY

www.12StoryLibrary.com

Copyright © 2019 by 12-Story Library, Mankato, MN 56003. All rights reserved. No part of this book may be reproduced or utilized in any form or by any means without written permission from the publisher.

12-Story Library is an imprint of Bookstaves.

Photographs ©: Aaron M. Sprecher/Associated Press, cover, 1; Keith Allison/CC2.0, 4; Arturo Pardavila III/CC2.0, 5; Tim Johnson/Associated Press, 6; Nathan K. Martin/Associated Press, 7; Lance Cpl. Sarah Wolff-Diaz/US Marine Corps, 8; Frank Boxler/Associated Press, 9; Kris Krüg/CC2.0, 10; Hakandahlstrom/CC3.0, 11; alarico/Shutterstock.com, 11; s_bukley/Shutterstock.com, 12; RICHARD DREW/Associated Press, 13; Focus on Sport/Getty Images, 14; David Durochik/Associated Press, 15; Suyk, Koen/CC3.0, 16; Lothar Spurzem/CC2.0, 17; PD, 18; The White House/PD, 19; Henry Bucklow/Lazy Photography/CC3.0, 20; Kasey Mueller/CC2.0, 21; Charles Rex Arbogast/Associated Press, 22; Chitose Suzuki/Associated Press, 23; ALFRED/DPPI-SIPA/Associated Press, 24; Andy Rogers/CC2.0, 25; Christopher Levy/Cal Sport Media/Associated Press, 26; Patrice Lapointe/ZUMA Press/Newscom, 27; PD, 28; Georg Pahl/Bundesarchiv, picture 102-11013A/CC3.0, 29

ISBN
978-1-63235-577-5 (hardcover)
978-1-63235-631-4 (paperback)
978-1-63235-692-5 (ebook)

Library of Congress Control Number:

Printed in the United States of America
Mankato, MN
July 2018

About the Cover

New York Yankees pitcher Mariano Rivera in 2013.

Access free, up-to-date content on this topic plus a full digital version of this book. Scan the QR code on page 31 or use your school's login at 12StoryLibrary.com.

Table of Contents

R0456091142

Mo Rivera Becomes Baseball's Greatest Closer

Mariano (Mo) Rivera was born in Panama in 1969. His father was a fisherman. Rivera and his friends played baseball on the beach when the tide was low. They made their own gear. Carboard milk cartons became gloves. Tree branches became bats. Baseballs were taped-up wads of used fishing nets.

After high school, Rivera wanted to play baseball. He made the Panama Oeste team in 1990. He was a shortstop, but the team needed a pitcher. Rivera volunteered. A scout for the New York Yankees saw him play. Rivera moved to the United States and played in the minor leagues. He became a relief pitcher, taking over for other pitchers in the middle of a game.

Rivera pitched his first major league game in May 1995. The Yankees lost 10-0. They sent him back to the minors. A month later, his fastball reached 95 miles per hour. He returned to the majors.

Rivera played 19 seasons in MLB (Major League Baseball). He could turn a losing game into a winning one. His cool head and positive attitude made him one of the best relief pitchers ever to play the game. He's the only one to be named MVP (Most Valuable Player) of a World Series, a League Championship Series, and an All-Star Game. Rivera retired in 2013.

1,111
Mo Rivera's major league pitching appearances, a record among right-handed pitchers.

- Rivera grew up in Panama.
- He started as a shortstop but switched to pitching.
- He spent 19 years playing for the Yankees in MLB.

RETIRING A HISTORIC NUMBER

Mariano Rivera was the last player to wear the number 42 on his uniform. This had been baseball legend Jackie Robinson's number. When Rivera retired in September 2013, the Yankees officially retired the number.

2

Hakeem Olajuwon Finds the Dream in Houston

Olajuwon (34) makes a shot in the NBA playoffs in 1988.

Hakeem Olajuwon was born in 1963 in Nigeria. He grew up playing table tennis, soccer, and handball. At 15, he picked up basketball. Olajuwon didn't know the rules. But he was seven feet tall. The coach told him to just stand there and block everything.

Olajuwon earned a spot on the University of Houston team. He moved to Texas in 1981. He

FAITH AND BASKETBALL

Hakeem Olajuwon credits his faith for his success. A devout Muslim, he prayed regularly. He went to the mosque every Friday, even on the road. He fasted during Ramadan. He saw this as a time to focus on discipline and self-control. He brought those skills onto the court.

3,830

The NBA record for blocked shots, still held by Hakeem Olajuwon.

- Olajuwon was born and raised in Nigeria.
- He was a key player in the NBA for 18 years.
- He is in the Basketball Hall of Fame.

worked with NBA (National Basketball Association) star Moses Malone. Olajuwon helped the Cougars make it to the NCAA Final Four three years in a row.

Olajuwon was drafted onto the Houston Rockets. He worked on a different skill each summer. He developed the Dream Shake. This mix of head fakes, spins, and jump shots stumped defenders.

In April 1993, Olajuwon became an American citizen. In 1994 and 1995, the Rockets won the NBA championship. Olajuwon earned the MVP title both years. In 1996, he won Olympic gold with the American men's basketball team.

Olajuwon retired in 2002. The Rockets retired his No. 34 jersey that year. In 2008, Olajuwon entered the Naismith Memorial Basketball Hall of Fame. He was admired for his skills. He was also respected for his character.

Paula Newby-Fraser Races Her Way to Fame

Paula Newby-Fraser was born in 1962 in Zimbabwe. She grew up in South Africa. She played many sports, including swimming and field hockey. She enjoyed watching endurance sports. She started competing in triathlons. A triathlon combines swimming, cycling, and running into a single race. Newby-Fraser won the South African Triathlon in 1985.

That year, she raced in the Ironman World Championships in Hawaii for the first time. The Ironman is 2.4 miles (4 km) of swimming, 112 miles (180 km of cycling), and 26.2 miles (42 km) of running. Newby-Fraser came in third.

Newby-Fraser moved to San Diego, California. The next year, she won her first Ironman World Title. Starting in 1989, she won five in a row. In 1995, as she neared the end of the race, she collapsed. She was severely dehydrated. After drinking water, Newby-Fraser stood up and walked to the finish line. She came in fourth.

In 1996, Newby-Fraser won her eighth and final title. She dominated the race along the Kona coast. This earned her the nickname the Queen of Kona. In all, Newby-Fraser won 24 full-distance races. She is considered the most accomplished triathlete of all time.

Newby-Fraser is now a triathlon coach. She has helped hundreds of athletes. She helped create the Ironman coaching certification. Newby-Fraser uses modern technology. She also uses faith and passion for the sport.

THINK ABOUT IT

The Ironman is one of the world's most challenging races. Why do you think people do it? What is one way you would like to challenge yourself?

17

Years Paula Newby-Fraser's world-record Ironman time of 8 hours, 50 minutes, and 24 seconds stood unbroken.

- Newby-Fraser grew up playing sports in South Africa.
- She moved to San Diego, California, in 1985.
- She won eight Ironman World titles, the most of any triathlete.

Wayne Gretzky Brings Hockey Greatness to America

Wayne Gretzky was born in Ontario, Canada, in 1961. He grew up skating on a rink in his backyard. At five, he played hockey with kids twice his age. By 13, he had scored more than 1,000 goals.

Gretzky started playing for the Edmonton Oilers when he was 18. For nine years, he and the Oilers seemed unstoppable. In 1988, they won the league

playoffs. It was their fourth Stanley Cup win in five years.

The Oilers stunned the hockey world that August. They traded Gretzky to the Los Angeles Kings. Gretzky had just married American actress Janet Jones. He wanted to support his wife, her career, and their family. That meant moving to California.

Hockey was not yet popular in America. Signing the world's greatest hockey player to a US team changed that. In 1989, Gretzky earned the NHL (National Hockey League) MVP trophy for the ninth time. He spent seven years with the Kings. He led them to the playoffs five times. In 1993, they made it to the finals. They lost to the Canadiens.

Gretzky played his last three years with the New York Rangers. On April 18, 1999, he played his 1,487th and final NHL game. The NHL retired

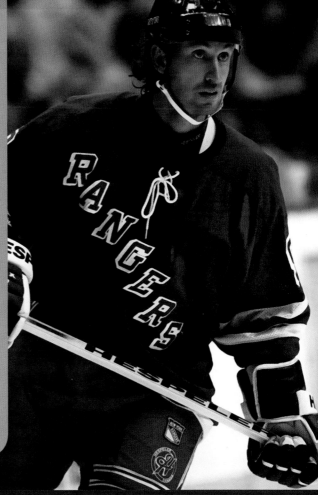

1,016

Goals Wayne Gretzky scored in the NHL, including both regular season and playoff games.

- Gretzky grew up playing hockey in Canada.
- He started playing for the Edmonton Oilers when he was 18.
- He was traded to the LA Kings after marrying an American.
- Gretzky helped make hockey popular in the United States.

Gretzky's number, 99. That June, Gretzky entered the Hockey Hall of Fame.

Gretzky left the NHL holding or sharing 61 records. His dominance earned him the nickname the Great One. There will never be another Gretzky, but his career inspired countless young hockey players.

Martina Navratilova Revolutionizes Tennis

tennis playing. At 15, she won the Czech national tournament. In 1973, at age 16, she turned pro. She started competing in the United States. She knew her career would be better if she lived in America. In 1975, after playing in the US Open, 18-year-old Navratilova defected.

She often faced American Chris Evert in major event finals. Evert won 21 of their first 25 matches. In 1981, Evert beat Navratilova 6-0, 6-0 in an important match. Navratilova knew something had to change.

She met basketball star Nancy Lieberman that day. She soon started a training program that Lieberman designed. Renée Richards helped her with strategy. Nutritionist Robert Haas created a diet for her. These advisors were dubbed Team Navratilova. They filled her guest box at matches. Other players made fun of this.

Martina Navratilova was born in 1956. She grew up in communist Czechoslovakia. Her stepfather, Mirek Navratil, introduced her to tennis. She later adopted a version of his last name.

Navratilova worked hard on

2,189

Total matches Martina Navratilova won, including singles and doubles.

- Navratilova grew up playing tennis in Czechoslovakia.
- She defected to the United States when she was 18.
- She revolutionized how tennis players train and eat.

OPENLY HONEST

In 1981, Navratilova became an American citizen. She also came out as a lesbian. Some people didn't support her. Navratilova didn't care. She didn't want to hide who she was. Being open brought her freedom. It made her a happier person and a better player.

In 1982, Navratilova won 90 matches. She lost only three. The following year, she won 86 and lost just one. In 1984, she won a record 74 matches in a row. Other tennis players noticed. Some started following similar eating and training programs. Months away from her 50th birthday, Navratilova won the US Open mixed doubles championship.

Football Gets a Kick from Jan Stenerud

Jan Stenerud was born in 1942 in Festund, Norway. Growing up, he spent his summers playing soccer. But he was a really good ski jumper. He earned a skiing scholarship to Montana State University.

The ski team trained by running up and down the football stadium steps. One afternoon in 1964, Stenerud saw kicker

Dale Jackson practicing on the field. Stenerud asked if he could try. He kicked a few with the side of his foot. He sent the ball farther than Jackson had. Then he went back to running the stairs.

A few weeks later, the football coach asked Stenerud to show him some kicks. After muffing his first try, Stenerud made several long kicks. He became the team's kicker in 1965. That year, Stenerud made a 59-yard (54 m) field goal. It was an NCAA record. It also beat the NFL (National Football League) record by three yards (2.7 m).

Stenerud joined the Kansas City Chiefs in 1967. His practice was six kicks on a Friday afternoon. He still made over 70 percent of his field goal attempts. Other kickers made less than 50 percent. Stenerud played with the NFL for 19 years. By 1985, he practiced 30-40 kicks three times a week. He made 90 percent of his attempts.

Stenerud's kicking revolutionized football. Straight-on kickers became obsolete. Kickoffs used to start at the 40-yard line. Because of Stenerud's long kickoffs, the NFL moved them to the 35-yard line.

Stenerud became an American citizen in 1976. In 1991, he was the first kicker to enter the Pro Football Hall of Fame.

1,699
Points Jan Stenerud scored while playing for the NFL.

- Stenerud grew up ski jumping in Norway.
- He switched from skiing to kicking at Montana State.
- He played in the NFL for 19 years.
- He revolutionized kicking in American football.

Mario Andretti Becomes the Driver of a Century

Mario Andretti was born in 1940 in a part of Italy that is now Croatia. After World War II, it became part of communist Yugoslavia. The Andretti family fled. From 1948 to 1955, they lived in a refugee camp in Lucca, Italy.

Car racing was popular in Italy. Mario and his twin, Aldo, were fans. In 1955, the Andrettis moved to Pennsylvania. The brothers found a racetrack nearby. They started racing in 1959. In two years, Mario won 20 races. Aldo got hurt and quit.

By 1964, Andretti had raced stock, midget, sprint, and Indy cars. He was really good in open-wheel cars. In 1965, he raced a full Indy season. Andretti earned Rookie of the Year. He was the youngest driver to win the Indy Car Championship.

Andretti won NASCAR's Daytona 500 in 1967. He also won the endurance race 12 Hours of Sebring in Florida. In 1968, Andretti made his Formula One debut. F1 is the world's premier open-wheel racing circuit.

Andretti won the F1 championship in 1978. He returned to American racing in the 1980s. In 1984, at age 44, he won his last Indy Car championship. In a unanimous vote, he was named Driver of the Year. In 2000, Andretti was named Driver of the Century.

111
Mario Andretti's racing wins in a career spanning five decades.

- Andretti spent much of his youth in a refugee camp in Italy.
- He fell in love with racing in Italy, but he started racing in America.
- He raced and won in a wide variety of vehicles.

A FAMILY AFFAIR

In the 1980s and 1990s, racing was an Andretti family affair. Mario Andretti started 10 races on the front line next to his son Michael. Sometimes there were four Andrettis on the track. Mario raced against his sons Michael and Jeff and his nephew John.

Andretti drove this Lotus in the 1969 German Grand Prix.

9

Phillip Dutton Leads the Way in Eventing

Phillip Dutton was born in Australia in 1963. He grew up on a farm with horses. From a young age, Dutton competed in horse riding events.

Dutton's specialty is eventing. This is like a triathlon for a horse and rider. A competition takes three days. Day one tests their dressage. This shows how well they can perform complicated movements. Day two tests their speed, endurance, and jumping ability. They ride over a four-mile (6.4-km) cross-country course. Day three tests their arena jumping.

Dutton moved to the United States in 1991 to train. He competed at the Olympics six times. In 1996, 2000, and 2004, he was on the Australian team. In 2006, Dutton became a US citizen. He competed on the American team in 2008, 2012, and 2016. At the 2016 Rio games, Dutton was the US team's oldest athlete. He was 52. He earned an individual bronze medal.

In 2009, Dutton helped form the Professional Riders Organization (PRO). It uses education and advocacy to improve the sport of eventing. Dutton and his wife, Evie, own and manage two farms. They help other riders and horses train.

Dutton's passion for equestrian eventing is clear. He and his horses

435

Points Phillip Dutton earned in international competition in 2017.

- Dutton grew up riding horses in Australia.
- He moved to America to train.
- He competed in six Olympics, three for each of his countries.
- He continues to share his knowledge and love of equestrian sport.

still rank among the best in the sport. Dutton finished his 2017 season ranked fourth. It was his third consecutive year as the top North American. An injury kept him from doing better.

Gao Jun Brings Serious Play to Ping-Pong

Gao Jun was born in China in 1969. She grew up watching table tennis on TV. In China, table tennis is an important sport. Gao started playing when she was five. She went to a boarding school for athletes. At 17, she won a spot on the Chinese National Team.

Gao played in the 1992 Barcelona Olympics. She won a silver medal

2009

Year Gao Jun was inducted into the USATT Hall of Fame.

- Gao started playing table tennis in China when she was five.
- She won a silver medal in doubles at the 1992 Barcelona Olympics.
- She represented America at three Olympics.
- She coaches young Americans in the sport.

THINK ABOUT IT

Some members of the US table tennis team felt Gao Jun should not have been allowed on the team. They felt she took opportunities away from them. What do you think?

in women's doubles. But China expected gold. In 1993, Gao played in the World Championships. She was the only Chinese player to make it to the final four. She lost the match. Gao stopped playing.

She moved to Maryland in 1994. A reporter asked if she would play for the United States. She didn't think so. At 25, she was old for the sport. Plus Americans don't take it seriously. They call it Ping-Pong. They play it for fun in their basements.

In 1997, Gao became an American citizen. USATT (USA Table Tennis) asked her to play for them. In 1999, Jun beat some highly-ranked players. This put her in the world's top 20. It qualified her for the 2000 Sydney Olympics. She represented America in the Olympics three times.

Today Gao trains America's promising young players. With her help, maybe table tennis will become big in America someday.

Khatuna Lorig
Draws Attention to Archery

Khatuna Lorig was born in 1974 in the Soviet Union. Her homeland is now the country of Georgia. Lorig started archery when she was 13. For eight months, she practiced holding a bow. Finally, she shot an arrow. It hit the target. The second arrow struck the first arrow.

Lorig competed in her first Olympics in 1992. The Soviet Union had collapsed the previous year. She competed on the Unified Team. This was a group of athletes from 12 former Soviet countries. Her archery team won the bronze medal.

Life in Georgia was tough. There was no electricity. Food was scarce. Lorig practiced in her basement by candlelight. She finished in 49th place at the 1996 Atlanta Olympics.

In Atlanta, Lorig fell in love with America. She moved to New Jersey and applied for citizenship. The wait was long. She competed on the Georgian team at the 2000 Sydney Olympics. She missed the Athens Olympics in 2004. She was still waiting for her new citizenship.

In 2005, Lorig became an American. She moved to California and started training at the US Olympic

Training Center in Chula Vista. She represented her new country at the 2008 Beijing Olympics. Her teammates chose her to carry the flag in the closing ceremonies. That was a great honor. Lorig competed for America again in the 2012 London Olympics.

In 2011, Lorig taught actress Jennifer Lawrence how to look like an expert archer. Lawrence played Katniss in the *Hunger Games* movies.

51

Draw weight of Khatuna Lorig's bow in pounds (23 kg).

- Lorig grew up in the Soviet Union.
- She has competed in five Olympics under three different flags.
- Her teammates chose Lorig to carry the US flag at the closing ceremonies of the Bejiing Olympics.

Maame Biney
Skates into History

44.305

Maame Biney's winning time for the 500-meter Junior World title, in seconds.

- Born in Ghana, Biney moved to America when she was five.
- She was the first black woman on a US speedskating team.
- She was the first American woman to win a Junior World Championship title in speedskating.

Maame Biney was born in Ghana in 2000. When she was five, she moved to the United States. She lived with her father near Washington, DC. Biney started taking figure skating lessons at age six. She was very fast on skates. So fast, her coach suggested she try speedskating.

Smarts and speed made Biney a natural at short track speedskating. She brought strength and fierceness to a sport with tight turns and close quarters.

In 2017, Biney moved to Salt Lake City to train. Her goal was to compete in the 2018 PyeongChang Olympics. She became the first

black woman to make the American speedskating team.

Biney's Olympic performance was disappointing. She didn't make it past the quarterfinals. She vowed to train harder. Just one month later, Biney became the first American woman to be a Junior World Champion. She dominated the 500-meter event at the 2018 World Junior Short Track Championship in Poland.

The young skater gets noticed for more than her speed on the ice. Her smile draws attention. So does her giggle. Biney doesn't want to be known as bubbly, though. She wants to be known as determined. She brings energy and enthusiasm to the American team. These are valuable qualities.

THINK ABOUT IT

Maame Biney never imagined she'd be a role model. Now she gets messages telling her she's an inspiration. What do you think makes a good role model?

James Naismith

We can thank Canada for basketball. James Naismith was born in Canada in 1861. He came to Massachusetts to study physical education. In 1891, he created a new indoor game. It used a ball, peach baskets, and 13 rules. Basketball is now one of the most popular games in the world.

Alex Findlay

The man who is called the father of American golf was born in Scotland in 1865. Alexander H. (Alex) Findlay came to the United States in 1887. While working on a ranch in Nebraska, he designed a six-hole golf course. He went on to design 130 courses and spread the gospel of golf throughout America.

Knute Rockne

American football was revolutionized by a Norwegian. Born in Norway in 1888, Knute Rockne moved to Chicago in 1893. He was a player and coach at Notre Dame. His plays stumped opponents. He designed uniforms with less bulk and more protection. He paved the way for modern football.

Sonja Henie

Another Norwegian brought star power to figure skating. Born in Norway in 1912, Sonja Henie competed for Norway in four Olympics. She won gold in three. In 1936, she moved to the United States. She starred in 11 Hollywood movies, showing off her skating talent. She toured the world in sold-out ice shows.

Editor's note:
America is a nation of immigrants. This series celebrates important contributions immigrants have made to sports. In choosing the people to feature in this book, the author and 12-Story Library editors considered diversity of all kinds and the significance and stature of the work.

Glossary

advocacy
The act of supporting
an idea or cause.

consecutive
Following one after another without
a break.

defect
To leave a country and its politics to
go to another.

dehydrated
Lacking needed water.

equestrian
Something related to riding horses.

muff
To miss a catch or
mess something up.

obsolete
No longer used; out
of date.

premier
The most important, leading, or best
of something.

promote
To support the growth or
development of something.

retire a number
To stop using a shirt number worn by
a particular player.

unanimous
Agreed to by everyone.

For More Information

Books

Bildner, Phil, and Brett Helquist. *Martina & Chrissie: The Greatest Rivalry in the History of Sports.* Somerville, MA: Candlewick Press, 2017.

Coy, John, and Joe Morse. *Hoop Genius: How a Desperate Teacher and a Rowdy Gym Class Invented Basketball.* Minneapolis, MN: Carolrhoda Books, 2013.

Herman, Gail. *Who Is Wayne Gretzky?* New York: Grosset & Dunlap, 2015.

Rivera, Mariano, Wayne R. Coffey, and Sue Corbett. *The Closer: Young Readers Edition.* New York: Little, Brown, 2014.

Visit 12StoryLibrary.com

Scan the code or use your school's login at **12StoryLibrary.com** for recent updates about this topic and a full digital version of this book. Enjoy free access to:

- Digital ebook
- Breaking news updates
- Live content feeds
- Videos, interactive maps, and graphics
- Additional web resources

Note to educators: Visit 12StoryLibrary.com/register to sign up for free premium website access. Enjoy live content plus a full digital version of every 12-Story Library book you own for every student at your school.

Index

About the Author

Janet Slingerland was an engineer before she started writing books. She lives in New Jersey with her husband, three children, and a dog. Her family tree includes many immigrants and a few athletes.

READ MORE FROM 12-STORY LIBRARY

Every 12-Story Library Book is available in many fomats. For more information, visit 12StoryLibrary.com